How To Grow Your Market, Brand, & Sales
With Mobile Apps

Written By Kyle D. Amaker
CEO at MobileFusionSoft.com, Inc

© 2016 by MobileFusionSoft.com, Inc
All Rights Reserved

COPYRIGHT NOTICE

© 2016 MobileFusionSoft.com, Inc. All Rights Reserved. Only the person who purchased this material is authorized to use any/all marketing and advertising content for his/her own use. These are copyrighted materials.

Any unauthorized transfer or license, use, photocopying or distribution of these materials to anyone else other than the licensed client/purchaser is strictly prohibited. Should anyone do so, they will be prosecuted to the fullest extent of the law.

All rights reserved under International Copyright Law. This publication may not be reproduced, stored in retrieval system, or transmitted in whole or in part, in any form or by any means, electronic, mechanical, photocopying, recording or otherwise, except for personal use, without prior express written permission of the publisher.

Published By:
MobileFusionSoft.com, Inc
P.O. Box 171
Williamstown, NJ 08094
Phone: 800-951-5632
Fax: 856-513-9752

The entire "**How To Grow Your Market, Brand, & Sales With Mobile Apps**" is proprietary to MobileFusionSoft.com, Inc. This is published work protected by federal copyright laws and no unauthorized copying, adaptation, distribution or display is permitted.

To God Be The Glory!

Isaiah 41:10

Fear thou not; for I am with thee; be not dismayed; for I am thy God: I will strengthen thee; yea, I will help thee; yea, I will uphold thee with right hand of my righteousness.

Table of Contents

Introduction 5

Chapter 1 – Understanding Mobile Apps 9
What Are Mobile Apps? 11
The History Of Mobile Apps 12
Today's App Culture 13

Chapter 2 – Why Do You Need A Mobile App 15
The World Has Gone Mobile 17
Mobile Apps Offer On-The-Go Marketing 17
It Can Be A Social Platform 18
Better Service And Sales 18
Real-Time Rich Data Capture 19
Apps Boost Interest 19
Increase Customer Engagement 19
Access It Even In The Middle Of The Night 20
A Larger, Younger Audience 20
Mobile Apps Are Very Convenient For Customers 20
People Spend More Time On Mobile Apps 21
Mobile Apps Help You Build Brand Loyalty 21
Apps Generate New Leads 22
Mobile Shopping Is On The Way Up 22
It Gives You An Edge Over Competition 23
The Most Powerful Marketing Medium Ever Invented! 24
Bring Customers In With Geo-Fencing 26
Loyal User Base 26
Reduce Support Costs 27
Increase Customer Satisfaction 27
Increase Sales 28
Final Thoughts 29

Chapter 3 – About Mobile Marketing 31
Mobile Marketing Empowers Your Business........................... 33
Enhance Your Marketing Efforts Though Mobile 33

Marketing Benefits Of Mobile Apps 33
Provide Instant Gratification 33
Rich Media Increase Engagement 34
Enables Deep Customization 34
Maximize Device Capabilities For Interactions 35
Visually Represents Brand Well.. 35
User Rich Experiences To Target & Attract People 36
Technical Capabilities Of Mobile Apps 36
Quickly Update Your Mobile App Content 36
Help People Find You Quickly And Easily With GPS 37
Excite Consumers With Mobile Apps.................................. 38

Features That Maximize Your App Effectiveness 39
Use Tell-A-Friend To Spread Your Message....................... 39
Trigger Phone Calls With A Single Press............................. 39
Leverage Your Existing Videos 40

The Best Strategy 40
Mobile Marketing For Small Businesses..............................41
Mobile Apps A Strategic Marketing Tool...........................44

Chapter 4 – Building Your Brand With Mobile Apps 47
About Mobile Apps...49
Mobile Apps Offer Limitless Communication Possibilities.49
Stay On Top Of Mind With Messaging................................49
Engage Users With Offers...50
Drive Purchases With Coupons 50
Enhance Messaging With Videos 50
Mobile App Brand Guidelines...51
Use High-End Graphics To Maximize Your Brand Image....51
Icons And Your Logo 52
Useful Tips For Successful Mobile App Branding 52

Chapter 5 – Increase Sales With Mobile Apps 55
Showcasing Products & Services 57
    Lure Consumers With A Mobile Product Showroom 57
    Capture Leads While Increasing Engagement 58
    The Power Of Push Notifications 59
    Collect Data For Profiling Further Marketing 61
    Befriend Social Networks To Reach More Consumers ... 63
    Mobile Apps Are The New Loyalty Cards 64
    Enter The Mobile App 65
    Making It Happen 66
    Sticky Apps Ensure Long-Term Success 67
    Ensure Stickiness And Success With These Strategies .. 68

Chapter 6 – Conclusion 71
Choosing A Mobile App Provider 73
Conclusion 74

Chapter 7 – About MobileFusionSoft.com, Inc 77
What We Do 79
Our Services 80

Industries We Service 81
    Car Dealerships 83
    Churches 84
    Fitness Clubs 85
    Hair Salons/Barber Shops 86
    Realtors 87
    Restaurants 88
    Retail 89
    Schools 90

App Functionality 91
    Around Us 93
    Contact 93
    Push Notifications 93
    Email Form 94
    Email Photo 94
    Events 94
    Events v2 95

Fan Wall 95
Food Ordering 95
Golf Courses 96
GPS Coupon 96
Image Gallery 96
Info-1-Tier 97
Info-2_Tier 97
Info-3-Tier 97
Loyalty 98
Mailing List 98
Membership 98
Menu 99
Merchandise 99
Mortgage Calculator 99
Music 100
News 100
Notepad 100
PDF 101
Podcast 101
QR Coupon 101
QR Scanner 102
Real Estate 102
Reservation 102
RSS Feed 103
Sports Stats 103
Tell Friend 103
Tip Calculator 104
Push Notifications 104
Voice Recording 104
WuFoo Form 105
YouTube Channel 105
One Touch Calling 105
Video Integration 106
Direction View 106
3RD Party Integrations 107

Request A Free Custom Mobile App Demo **109**

FAQ **111**

INTRODUCTION

Introduction

Welcome to How To Market, Brand, & Profit With Mobile Apps. This book provides an overview of how your business can effectively create mobile apps to improve brand recognition, boost lead generation, and increase customer engagement. As the popularity of smartphone apps widens among consumers of all generations, companies must address mobile marketing in order to succeed in the online and offline marketplace.

Consumers expect apps. Almost daily, the media reports on a new app innovation. Despite the powerful benefits mobile apps offer, most small businesses refrain from taking advantage of mobile opportunities. Usually it's because they don't understand the long-term possibilities or how to integrate mobile efforts into current campaigns.

Attitudes like these keep many from expanding their marketing reach and exploding their sales. They simple do not understand how versatile and effective mobile apps can be. Because they hesitate to develop the next "app for that", a competitor beats them to it.

Mobile apps have positioned themselves as the new-age marketing tools that help in launching a product or a company in the market, creating awareness, converting leads into business, engaging customers and creating a loyal customer and client base.

Technology has drastically changed the manner in which business is conducted these days. While there have been a number of customer engagement software available in the market, the mobile application market is booming exponentially; and is poised to transform business processes completely.

This book will cover the benefits of creating a mobile app as well as best practices for ensuring your app's success. We'll show you how to apply traditional marketing practices that you're already familiar with to mobile apps. We'll discuss how to customize apps so they enrich consumer and brand interactions, deliver specific and timely marketing messages, incorporate rich media to showcase products and services, and gather consumer data to enhance future campaigns.

In essence, this book will help you create a successful mobile apps and develop exciting new ideas for maximizing the effectiveness of your app with all your marketing campaigns, including promotions, loyalty programs, and social media.

If you have any mobile app development related questions or wish to set up a free no obligation consultation I am available! Please do no hesitate to contact me.

To Your Success!

Kyle Amaker

Kyle D. Amaker
CEO at MobileFusionSoft.com, Inc

CHAPTER 1

UNDERSTANDING MOBILE APPS

What Are Mobile Apps?

Mobile Applications, also called a mobile app, is an application designed and developed to run on small handheld mobile devices, such as smartphones, tablet computers, and other mobile devices. Mobile applications are usually available through various application distributions platforms that are operated by the owners of the operation system. Such as the iTunes's App Store for Apple's iOS operating system and Google Play Store for Google's Android operating system.

Mobile applications are usually downloaded from the application distribution platforms to the target device. Although there are a number of advantages of using mobile applications, there are however, three major uses of mobile applications – the volume of information available to uses, the speed at which information can be accessed and advertising.

Mobile apps are usually offered for retrieving information and improving the general productivity of users such as emails, calendars, weather information, contacts and stock market information. However these days, mobile apps have ventured beyond basic services and are now offering mobile games, location-based services, order-tracking services, banking, medical apps, and ticket purchases. Although a number of mobile apps are free to download, a few of the apps have to be brought.

The mobile app world is exploding – literally. It is generating revenue, creating an expansive customer base, and providing faster and reliable access to large quantities of information. A large portion of our interactions is happening on mobile devices. Therefore, it is natural for businesses to look at the world of mobile applications to stay competitive and relevant in this technology- enabled world.

Businesses have, traditionally, been building their operational and strategic foundations on paper based processes. Although these paper-based development processes were efficient; they, however, almost always, showed slower turnaround times, errors and provided very poor visibility. However, these days, businesses are building and deploying mobile applications by keeping up with technological changes and innovation in the mobile market. The future of the business world, arguably, lies in developing mobile applications.

The History Of Mobile Apps

The extent to which mobile apps and mobile communication has integrated into our daily lives is astonishing, so much so that we feel quite uneasy and irritated when we have to spend a few minutes away from our smartphones and our daily dose of mobile apps. However, longtime users of mobile phones would vouch for the fact that until a few years ago there was nothing more than the classic "snake" game, calendar, and calculators that their mobile phone offered.

As soon as the technological boom happened, mobile app developers started making room for smartphones to carry games, health care tips, weather reports, ticket booking portals, and much more. With consumers constantly demanding faster, better, feature-rich application, mobile networks started growing and mobile handset manufacturers started going into overdrive mode by accepting new and advanced applications from outside developers. That is when software developers saw a huge potential to capitalize on the needs on the consumers by offering them faster, technically advanced, and user-enriched apps.

The major surge in the mobile application world came with the release of Apple's very first iPhone. However, others soon started joining the app race, and together are flooding the market with innumerable mobile applications. This ballooning market trend had made sure that consumers are flooded with large companies such as Apple, Google, Samsung, Nokia, and others are offering a well developed and sustainable software application ecosystem with a variety of application.

Today's App Culture

Until a few years ago, it was widely assumed that the app market would soon see a decline and that there would be stagnation in the app market. Moreover, everyone started wondering what else was there for the app market to develop. Every idea and every app, that could possibly be conceived was designed, developed and dusted! Or so everyone thought!

The mobile application count has, in fact, seen an upward spike over the years. According to recent popular research reports, the number of apps had doubled between 2014 and 2015 and has, in fact, tripled since then. It is not only big names such as Facebook, Twitter, Instagram, and Snapchat that are hogging the app limelight, a number of small-time and new developers have understood the pulse of consumers and are using innovative solutions aimed at improving the overall mobile experience of users.

The mobile activity has slowly taken over desktop activity. Research shows that mobile app adoption is growing way faster then web adoption did in 1900s. In fact, at least 44% if cell phones users have kept their mobile phones by their side even when they slept, just to make sure that they do not miss a single notification.

CHAPTER 2

WHY DO YOU NEED A MOBILE APP

With mobile apps developed for mobile operating systems from Apple, Android, and others, you can create brand awareness and loyalty among a huge number of existing and potential customers. In fact, many customers now expect a business or brand to have its own dedicated mobile app. This means that it is not only becoming a necessity to gain a competitive edge over other businesses, it is becoming a necessity to avoid falling behind your competition. Having a dedicated mobile app adds to the credibility of the brand.

Keeping in mind the importance that mobile applications hold in today's society, it is only wise to create one for your business. Here are the top reasons why your business needs a mobile app.

The World Has Gone Mobile

There is no denying that the world has gone mobile and there is no turning back. Consumers are using their smartphones to find local businesses. Your online branding efforts are being viewed via mobile channels. Thus, just having a website is not enough anymore. Users are turning away from the desktop browsers and relying on mobile applications. Unlike traditional websites, which overwhelm your 6-inch mobile screen, apps thrive as an intuitive purchasing and browsing alternative.

Mobile Apps Offer On-The-Go Marketing

With mobile applications your existing customers can access your business anywhere and at any time in a user-friendly environment. Regular use of your app will reinforce your brand or business. This means that when they need to purchase something, chances are they will come to you. You have created a relationship with them using the app and this is tantamount to placing your business in your customers' pockets.

It Can Be A Social Platform

It almost goes without mentioning that people are obsessed with social media. So you will want to be a part of their obsessions well. Integrating social features such as comments, likes, in-app messaging and so forth in your app can help your business improve its social standing. People spend a lot of time on social media, especially Facebook, Twitter, and Instagram.

So by having a mobile application that gives them all the features they get in social media means that they'll spend more time in your app. This way, users are able to review, share or discuss products. Remember we are by nature social beings and mobile app development is the future of social interaction. A great example of this is Amazon.com that has essentially built its own community within its reviews area.

Better Service and Sales

Thankfully mobile app development has made sales easier than ever before. It is changing the way people buy and sell products and services. It has also changed the way customers view and analyzes a product before purchasing. This means that consumers have more options than ever to make informed buying decisions. With that said, it is important that you provide your client with a dedicated app, focused on providing customers with the information they are looking for. Don't forget that better service is one of the best practices to drive more sales. Mobile apps are perfect for service and support.

Real-Time Rich Data Capture

A mobile application saves you from the slow process of collecting data and analyzing it. Focus groups can be expensive and time consuming. Mobile apps make it easy to capture information about customer preferences and actions on your app. This information can be used to deliver personalized content that is relevant to the individual consumer as well as for making decisions on how to improve your app based on how customers are actually using it. Make sure you give your users the option to opt-in to a data program and explain to them that it will be used to improve their customer experience. Once they have given you their trust, don't disappoint them.

Apps Boost Interest

When you develop an application, it provides you an easy way to display your products or services to your existing and prospective customers. Each time they want to purchase something, they can simply use it as one-stop point to get all the information they need. And whenever you update the content, you can notify them and they can get the first glimpse of the new products or services you have on offer. This invites and tempts customers to check out your app on a regular basis.

Increase Customer Engagement

Engagement is exactly what you can create with your application. It ensures that your business is right in the palm of your customer's hand. Consumers can interact with your business while in the car, in the dentist waiting room and in line at the bank. Furthermore, you can use their location and profile information to personalize your offers in order to make them more relevant and attractive.

Access It Even In The Middle Of The Night

A mobile app can be accessed from anywhere at any time. Consumers can interact with your business while on the go. For example, they cannot only place additional orders but can access all account information, track recent sales and account activity. Business can also respond immediately to customer requests. This level of service takes your business to the next level in your customers' minds.

A Larger, Younger Audience

Most young people went mobile a long time ago. Almost 75% of the millennial generation will have smartphones by the end of the year. It is hard to engage the younger generation using outdated techniques. Young people choose to rely on their mobile devices, even though they may have access to a traditional PC. Smartphones have become the new tool for chatting with friends, browsing and purchasing products and services online. To reach this audience, you need to have a mobile app.

Mobile Apps Are Very Convenient For Customers

Mobile applications are easier to use than websites. Apps are usually designed with primary focus on usability. In fact, apps were for the most part designed to offer the next level of usability. The benefits are even greater when businesses decide to develop a custom mobile app that allow more flexibility and can address specific customer needs. Once installed, that application will help your customers reach your support team, your services and the payment section. The professionalism you show will increase trust and recognition by your targeted audience through your app.

People Spend More Time On Mobile Apps

You might be surprised to hear that mobile users spend 89 percent of the time that they're consuming mobile media in apps. That amounts to 29.5 hours for men every month, and almost 31 hours for women. It also leaves a measly 11 percent for mobile web browsing. It's enough to make you wonder why so many businesses have mobile optimized websites, but haven't even considered making an app. If you don't have an app, chances are that people aren't interacting with your company when they reach for their smartphone.

This makes sense when you realize that a whopping 85 percent of people in the United Kingdom, United States, Germany, France, India and Japan prefer mobile apps to mobile websites. These corporate programs are so popular because they're easier to navigate, more responsive and more convenient. No wonder an expected 4.4 billion mobile users will use apps by 2017.

Mobile Apps Help You Build Brand Loyalty

Mobile users often visit a website and never give it a second thought. However, when they make the effort to download an app they're already engaged with a brand. You can capitalize on this engagement and develop a real relationship and brand loyalty through your app. Include an easy way for customers to offer feedback on the app, your business, and their experiences interacting with your firm. Listening to people's likes and dislikes gives a valuable insight into what you're doing right and what you need to do better.

Sending targeted, personalized communication to your app users will make them feel special and drive sales. You can also use these engaged consumers for research about new products and developments.

Apps Generate New Leads

Most businesses think of apps as a great way to connect with their existing customers, but they're overlooking their lead-generating potential. One of the most popular app stores sees customers downloading more than 800 apps every second. This rapid uptake points to the public's insatiable app appetite.

Connected individual's love browsing through app stores and seeing what's new. If your app offers users real value, people will want to use it, even if they were previously unfamiliar with your brand. In this way a well-designed app can actually introduce a mobile user to your company and turn someone unfamiliar with your firm into a loyal fan.

Mobile Shopping Is On The Way Up

Ever since the rise of the smartphone in the late-2000s, the market penetration and demand for mobile devices has skyrocketed. Approximately one in five people around the world own a smartphone. That's an estimated 22 percent of the global population.

Half of all shoppers say they've used an app to make a purchase, and the majority of these are young people. If your company looks to appeal to youthful consumers, it's worth noting that almost half of the youthful consumers say they prefer making in-app purchases to using web-based shops.

It's not just people who'd prefer to shop in their pajamas driving the mobile shopping trend either. About a quarter of online orders are collected, rather than shipped, thanks to the rise of click-and-collect.

It Gives You An Edge Over Your Competition

As we learned earlier, more than seven out of every ten businesses don't have a mobile app. If you do, you're offering potential customers and loyal patrons something that your competitors aren't.

Differentiating yourself in your business sector has always been one of the most effective ways to unseat your rivals. Creating an app is a great way to appear more tech savvy and give your company the competitive edge it's been looking for, especially if you're attempting to appeal to an ever-connected demographic of youthful consumers.

It is nearly impossible to stand out in a crowd of well over a million. As of July 2015, Android users, for example, were able to choose more from than 1.6 million applications. Apple Store is the second largest app store after Play Store with over 1.5 million apps. It is important that your app stands out from the rest. However, making your product stand out in a saturated market is not as easy as you think.

While there are a lot of tricky gimmicks that you can try to make your app noticeable, you need to involve the user from the beginning in order to succeed. You have to make sure your item is user-friendly – before anything else. Users are attracted to apps that can provide them with what they really want.

The Most Powerful Marketing Medium Ever Invented!

Mobile apps are set to transform the manner in which business process have been conducted so far, so you should make sure that your business is not left behind in this race.

With the manner in which mobile devices have occupied every section of the society, it is natural that mobile devices will be the next place where most of the business processes are going to be conducted. Clearly, mobile apps will be designed by businesses to take care of their internal processes and also to have a competitive advantage over others very soon.

With the sheer number of mobile devices exploding in the market, the extent to which the wireless and wired networks have grown in the recent past and the fact that there are umpteen number of private and public clouds to help you with your data storage needs, the time to use mobile applications to improve your companies productivity has come. However, some small-scale companies are still wondering whether mobile apps are needed when they have their own website.

It is true that both mobile websites and mobile apps have their own respective needs and advantages; however, the time has come to really take a closer look at both and figure out which is best.

Mobile apps are fast becoming more popular that browser based websites. In 2015, people spent more than 20 minutes per day on browser based websites than mobile apps. However, by the end of 2015, the scenario changed completely, with the users spending more than 20 minutes on mobile apps than on browser based websites. So what makes mobile apps a better business plan than browser based websites.

There are some basic principles that vary between pure mobile websites and pure mobile apps. Pure mobile websites can be accessed through browsing while mobile apps can access after the installation process. Browser based sites offer static navigational user interface that might be very helpful for your business needs, while a mobile apps offers interactive user interface that helps business enjoy real-time data. Browsers require an Internet connection while mobile apps can be used even when you are offline.

Mobile apps offer high functionality and enable customers to perform a task easily such as paying bills, tracking payments and more whereas websites – both mobile and desktop – make sure that customers take some sort of immediate action like calling a business or making a purchase.

Finally, if you have enough resources, you can build and capitalize on both these platforms. However, if you are a small business or trying to venture into the world of mobile applications and websites only now, then you might consider the right platform depending on your audience and your business goals.

As a last word, mobile apps seem to be the future of the business and if you do not wish to be left out, you have to immediately take action and start working on developing your first business mobile app.

Bring Customers In With Geo-Fencing

By definition: Geo-fencing (geofencing) is a feature in a software program that uses the global positioning system (GPS) or radio frequency identification (RFID) to define geographical boundaries. A geofence is a virtual barrier.

In simple terms, geo-fence push notifications are a way for small businesses to send extremely targeted messages to their customers.

For example, a restaurant could section off an area of a competitor, and when a customer passes through this designated area a message would instantly send to the customer in an attempt to lure them over to the other restaurant with a special promotion. You can also just set them up around your business to notify customers when they're close and present them with an offer they can't refuse.

Loyal User Base

Everyone has the experience of using an app with lots of bugs and errors, complexities, frustrating interactions and unexpected behaviors. The truth is that, a poorly designed application reduces customer loyalty.

Users won't have a high tolerance for unstable applications and nothing can turn them away faster than a bad first impression. You may not be able to foster a lasting relationship with users.

On the contrary, a good user experience can create the kind of loyalty that keeps people coming back for more, increasing engagement. Giving users a reason to return by being engaging and useful is one of the ways to enhance UX and encourage member loyalty. This leaves a positive first impression on the user and gives them a sense of value for having downloaded your app.

Reduce Support Costs

A well-designed app can save you money and time. Consumers regularly struggle with simple issues that solutions can easily be found on a well-designed app. Mobile applications give customers a way to not only find solutions but to connect with your business 24/7, irrespective of where they are. They can offer direct personal calls with sales people, access to a help desk, live chat and even provide on-going support to customers.

You can save a lot of money, as you do not need to hire as many help desk staff. Also, users won't waste as much time asking for help. The app can provide all the information a customer needs on your company and products instantly, and in turn, will result in a higher level of engagement with your brand.

Increased Customer Satisfaction

Customer satisfaction is one of the keys to running a successful business. Success in any industry is often measured by the number of satisfied customers. The better experience you provide for your clients, the more satisfied they would be – and the opposite is true.

The worse experience you create for your customers, the more frustrated they will become with your offering. They will rarely recommend your product to their friends and relatives. The same applies to mobile applications.

If people do not like your app or do not use it, chances are users' expectations aren't being met or not enough value is being offered. So if you make an app that frustrates or annoys those, chances are your application will be deleted and get bad reviews.

The most common reason why users might abandon or delete an app is poor user experience. This includes heavy battery usage, slow responsiveness, too many ads and so forth. If an app can't provide a positive first impression, it is probably going to frustrate users and it is likely going to be deleted.

Increased Sales

A well-designed app will have increased traffic, transactions, and conversations. These apps will attract and keep more clients who will buy more products and leave positive feedback. Happy customers often spread the word to their friends and families. Users won't share your app if it fails to meet their expectations.

They also review your application online, which plays an important role in convincing other potential users to download the application. Also, the reviews reflect the current user satisfaction with the application. Remember online reviews are trusted sources of information, and building trust with users is a key component in ensuring that more people download and use the app.

Providing a great experience helps promote positive word of mouth, thereby increasing sales. Again, it leads to increased customer satisfaction and loyalty, and thus repeat business. User-centered designed also minimizes the number of bug fixes and maintenance needs that often surfaces after launching an app. Identifying glitches in advance can save tons of money on app updates in the future.

Final Thoughts

A well-thought-through mobile solution needs to conform to your overall digital strategy, offering a seamless and unmatched user experience. This means that the functionality and content that are delivered on your app must be in line with what your target audience actually wants. Regardless of the function or purpose of your app, the end product must provide a superior quality user experience. If you are unable to provide a quality mobile experience, you could be doing more harm than good to your reputation.

CHAPTER 3

ABOUT MOBILE MARKETING

Mobile Marketing Empowers Your Business

Mobile marketing enables you to more accurately target your marketing messages to a select audience. Unlike TV, web, and print, mobile apps gather consumer information that allow for greater specificity in promoting your brand, For example, you can target promotions to a person's particular preference, location, or time of day. The advancements in and proliferation of smartphones increase opportunities for mobile marketing. Because people take their phones everywhere, you can reach them 24/7.

Enhance Your Marketing Efforts Through Mobile

Today, most mobile marketing is delivered in three ways: SMS, mobile web, and mobile apps. Since all three methods offer their own unique set of advantages, they are most effective when combined with each other. The book, however, focuses solely on mobile apps and illustrates how apps can improve your marketing success with your target audiences.

Marketing Benefits Of Mobile Apps

Provide Instant Gratification

Since an app is installed on a consumer's device, all your functionality as well as the bulk of your graphics and content will reside on the device. This allows your app to always be available for immediate use; the consumer doesn't have to wait for long downloads every time he wants to access your content.

Today's media-oriented consumers are accustomed to having instant access to rich media on their television sets, DVD players, video game systems, tablets, and mobile phones. Apps uphold this expectation while providing rich, customized content.

> **"If You Can Imagine It, You Can Probably Create It"**

Rich Media Increases Engagement

Mobile apps allow you to develop highly customized, rich media experiences that engage mobile users. Building audio, video, photos, graphics, and text that effectively communicate your brand and marketing message is sometimes no possible on a mobile site. A custom mobile app is designed to incorporate all of these types of media to offer the richest experience possible.

Enables Deep Customization

Creating your own app lets you customize both content as well as look and feel. If you can imagine it, you can probably create it. Apps offer many options for designing custom screens, functionality, and experiences. Custom apps provide the same high-quality delivery of a television commercial, video game, or a very rich online experience. Since you know your audience's demographics, psychographics, and other characteristics, you can create apps that match your users' preferences.

Maximize Device Capabilities For Interactions

Since the release of the iPhone in 2007, Apple and its competitors have added sophisticated new device functions that are now considered standard. Examples: GPS, high-resolution camera lenses, accelerometers, high-resolution touch screens, and faster processors. Your business can take advantage of these phone capabilities as they developed high-quality, sophisticated apps that perform like computer programs.

These technical improvements provide significant marketing benefits by allowing companies to create interactive messaging that persuades the viewer to take action. Touch screens, in particular, heighten user engagement as mobile app users move their fingers across the screen.

Likewise, high-resolution displays increase user satisfaction with photo and movie media. GPS creates the potential to lead viewers right to the nearest store.

> **"Communicate A Brand's Message Quickly And Effective While Dazzling Them With Richness"**

Visually Represents Brand Well

Due to rich media and technical advances in smartphones, brands can take advantage of high-quality graphics, photos, videos, and audio that display well on high-resolution mobile screens. Gone are the days when apps from different industries typically looked the same due to device constraints. For example, a serious financial app might have appeared similar to an entertainment app.

Now, creative possibilities are staggering.

Use Rich Experiences To Target And Attract People

With the technical bar having been raised by Apple and other smartphone manufacturers and software developers, people now expect visually stunning mobile apps. The multimedia components in an app need to communicate a brand's message quickly and effectively while dazzling them with richness. It's the potential for interaction and the great content that keep them coming back for more.

The Technical Capabilities Of Mobile Apps

Understanding the technical capabilities of mobile apps will help you create applications that boost consumer engagement and encourage desired consumer behaviors. Smartphones, especially the iPhone and Android models, offer numerous opportunities to use built-in functions and make your app fun to use as you accomplish your marketing goals.

> **"People Now Expect Visually Stunning Mobile Apps"**

Quickly Update Your Mobile App Content

You can easily and quickly change text, graphics and videos on our server that immediately updates content within the mobile app. This ensures users always receive your newest content and messaging. And because content in loaded over the network, you don't have to rebuild the app or wait through app approval cycle to send our promotions and other critical marketing messages. This powerful ability lets you send periodic product or service tips as well as your latest offers to enhance your brand and increase user excitement during promotions or contests.

You benefit by avoiding redeployment of your app or having to obtain app store approvals for changes.

> **"Enhance Your Brand And Increase User Excitement During Promotions Or Contests"**

Consider asking your app user to take a photo of a visit to your business. For instance, someone could place a photo taken on their phone and upload all within the app.

You can also launch a photo contest with prizes and awards for the most creative photo of your product. To make the contest even more fun, ask loyalty club members to act as contest judges and feature winners on your Facebook company page.

> **"Think Of Ways You And Your Customers Can Use Photos"**

Help People Find You Quickly And Easily With GPS

You'll want to consider location awareness, a powerful feature using built-in GPS for your app.

With Apple, Google, and other map programs, you can offer users quick directions and phone numbers for local retail stores. In fact, many smartphones have speech-to-text capability, making it even faster for consumers to find information and store locations quickly.

Excite Consumers With Mobile Apps

You can use apps to increase excitement and involvement with mobile users. And when consumers become excited and involved, they're more likely to share their experiences with friends and family through email, social networking, and other communication channels. With mobile apps, quite often there's a viral effect that boosts marketing response to your offers.

Imagine a sports car enthusiast who downloads an interactive car app. He engages with the app by changing the car's color or interior look.

He visually sits in the front seat and drives with the gearshift. He watches a video about the care embedded in the app, gets excited about the experience, want additional information, and schedules a test drive. Then he shares his enthusiasm with friends through social networks, email, or text messages.

> "Mobile Apps Offer Businesses Powerful Opportunities To Engage Consumers With Brands At All Hours In A Very Personal Way"

That's only one example of an interactive mobile app's power that is challenging, if not impossible, to duplicate with other media. Most consumers today expect rich media experiences. They use their phones to find information, play games, exchange photos with friends, locate retail stores, make phone calls, and more.

Because consumers typically keep their phones within nine feet of their bodies 24/7, especially when they're out and about, mobile apps offer businesses powerful opportunities to engage consumers with brands at all hours in a very personal way.

> "You Can Use Apps To Increase Excitement And Involvement With Mobile Users"

Features That Maximize Your App's Effectiveness

Use Tell A Friend To Spread Your Message

Most people enjoy sharing their positive experiences about products and services. "Tell a Friend," embedded in mobile apps, makes it easy for app users to send emails with prepopulated subjects and body text.

Senders only need to enter the recipient's name, encouraging friends, family, and others to check out the product or service.

> "Users Tell Their Friends About Products And Service They'd Love..."

Trigger Phone Calls With A Single Press

Mobile offers one of the most effective ways to share retail locations, directions, and phone numbers with consumers. In fact, someone who's highly interested in a product or service can quickly get additional information.

The app can trigger a phone call with just one button press, making it very easy for consumers to jump on a promotion.

Leverage Your Existing Videos

Consumers love streaming video. It is one of the most popular forms of mobile media. By inserting videos and other multimedia elements inside your apps, you offer a richer media experience, enhancing positive views about your products and services.

If you have available video content from your television campaigns or online channels, consider leveraging it within your app to increase user interest.

The Best Strategy

Do you have products or services that need exposure? Are you trying to determine how to sell and market them while saving on advertising costs at the same time? Then traditional advertising such as billboards, newspaper and television ads are not going to help you reach your goal. Consider implementing a **mobile marketing** strategy.

Mobile marketing is the best method for providing you with more clients and more profit for less cost. So, you might ask yourself why **mobile marketing** is considered the best strategy to promote your business. Today, in over 30 countries, mobile phones have exceeded the 100% device to population ratio. Studies have proven that mobile phones are one of the most influential devices found today.

According to current predictions, the number of mobile phone subscriptions will continue to grow. So, what does this mean? Well, if you choose mobile as your advertising channel, you'll be able to expand your reach to the most possible prospects. Mobile is engaging, personal and can change the way you market your business. Don't you want your business strategy to include more profits for less cost?

Mobile marketing is the most practical marketing solution today. It's a fact that people often have their phone within arms-reach. This means that when you send an advertisement, your consumers are almost sure to read them. Put your company front of mind and you give your products and services a chance to shine.

So what's required? An effective message. Consider that a large client base with a message that provides no value to the consumer is pointless. Make your advertisement simple, catchy and most of all, truthful. Do not mislead your customer as your reputation is at stake. At this point, if you're a beginner in mobile, try to seek a professional to help you improve your advertising with **mobile marketing**.

Mobile Marketing For Small Businesses

Small businesses need all the advertising they can get, but jumping from one strategy to another without ensuring that they'll get results is pointless. Funds are limited and they need to make sure that whatever marketing campaign they pursue, they'll get a return on their investment.

The most common advertising campaign for small businesses is print (flyers, posters, and business cards). One form of marketing that they really need to look into as soon as possible is **mobile marketing**.

This form of marketing has several facets and we'll discuss them below:

1. **Mobile Apps**

   Because they are downloaded and installed, dedicated mobile apps can give your business the advantage of greater presence on customer devices. Mobile apps can give you more control, with features such as geo-targeted push notifications that alert device owners when they're near your business, and data collection capacities that help you personalize your marketing.

   In addition, mobile apps are easier to access on devices, and can help to streamline marketing strategies such as text-based loyalty programs and single-platform mobile payments.

2. **Mobile Websites**

   This is the most prevalent and fastest selling **mobile marketing** strategy to date. With the rising number of mobile devices available in the market and the increased number of mobile Internet users, premium mobile websites are a must for any small business that wants to be "on the map".

   Studies show that if a customer arrives on a business website that is not mobile optimized, they take it as an indication of the business not caring. If you want to get an idea how the scale of potential customers, look outside and take note of every individual currently on their mobile device.

3. **SMS Campaigns**
   When your phone beeps with an incoming notification, you'll surely check it and read the message. That's how direct and straightforward SMS marketing is. You'll build your SMS list, start text-to-win campaigns or send useful information to your current and prospective clients. Reach consumers anywhere, anytime!

4. **Mobile Loyalty Card**
   The Mobile Loyalty Card is the basis of loyalty marketing and is also a great way to increase sales, deliver a better customer experience, improve brand awareness and build a better relationship with your customers.

   Offer your customers coupons, discounts and deals just for being a regular. Mobile Loyalty programs can be used with other proximity marketing technologies such as beacons to send personalized messages to your consumer in real-time when they pass by a specific location.

5. **QR Codes**
   A QR code can be printed on an ad, in a newspaper or flyer. Once scanned, the user is directed to a specific URL or your virtual business card that can include your business phone number and email address. QR codes can be programmed to link the person who scanned it to automatic opt-in to your email or SMS list.

   Another beneficial feature of QR codes is their ability to geographically monitor the effectiveness of your campaigns. Meaning, you'll know where, when, and how your codes are scanned. It's useful for monitoring and managing your marketing strategies.

Your small business can employ any or all of these **mobile marketing** strategies to market your products or services. Further research will give you insights as to functionality of these campaigns, individually or as a complement. These marketing techniques are essential if you're working with a competent and knowledgeable marketer that genuinely cares for and believes in your products and services.

Mobile Apps A Strategic Marketing Tool

Industry experts see mobile apps as a viable strategic marketing tool. The primary motivation for many business owners is to adopt a mobile marketing strategy that enables their workforce to improve their productivity and ensures smooth operations. Although this is the current scenario, it seems that mobile apps are being used for more than just internal business processes purposes.

In fact, the ability of the mobile environment to connect to a number of customer groups is becoming more and more important. Any mobility strategy that your business might come up with has to consider two distinctly different scenarios with two distinct user groups, their needs and requirements. In addition to catering to the needs of the internal users, mobile apps and mobility strategy also caters to the needs of external users as well.

Mobile apps are considered as strategic marketing tools because they help you maximize your return on investment very easily.

In fact, mobile apps are known to:

- Help you position your brand or company in the market. An array of attractive mobile apps can help you position your brand as one of the market leaders; and help you build a competitive advantage over others.

- Mobile apps also help businesses reach out to their target audiences more easily. These easy to use mobile apps, available over multiple platforms, help you connect with a large customer base.

- Mobile apps help in converting leads into sales very easily. In fact, each app download can be considered as a conversion.

- Mobile apps help in efficient and effective customer engagement strategies. Mobile applications are know to be effective in bringing better interaction between customers and businesses.

- Once the mobile app is downloaded, it becomes a very valuable piece of real estate on your customer's device. It becomes a driver for customer loyalty and engagement.

CHAPTER 4

BUILDING YOUR BRAND WITH MOBILE APPS

About Mobile Apps

Similar to software installed on a desktop computer, Mobile Apps are software that is stored and run on a mobile device. This allows the software to take advantage of the capabilities provided by the mobile device it runs on. From consumers' standpoints, apps offer instant gratification. They see an icon for an application directly on their mobile device. Then they select that icon, the application immediately and is ready for their use.

> **"People Carry Their Smartphones Everywhere They Go"**

Mobile Apps Offer Limitless Communication Possibilities

Mobile apps offer almost unlimited capabilities. As long as your target handsets support it, you can deliver virtually anything. This benefit, along with mobile's highly personal nature, renders it a critical tool for business owners. People carry their smartphones everywhere they go. GPS capabilities further facilitate interaction between your message and the viewer.

Plus, when you send messages, smartphones also allow consumers to respond immediately through a simple button press. When they press it, behavioral profiles and analytics are delivered to your company.

Stay On Top Of Mind With Messaging

Keep consumers turned to your brand by inserting standard messages, photos, graphics or videos within the app, then updating them with new information whenever you wish. Note that sending messages at regular intervals is more important than the number of messages you send. In fact, too many messages may turn off mobile app users. So always consider why you're sending a message and its value to the receiver.

Engage Users With Offers

Exciting new offers keep app users engaged, causing them to return to your app more frequently to check out the latest promotions from your brand. You don't always have to offer substantial product discounts to attract users. Just send them on a regular basis and make them fun and engaging.

Drive Purchases With Coupons

Most people enjoy receiving discount coupons to purchase products or services. You might even try a theme. For example, during holidays or special events, consider sending a coupon related to that theme. If you're an athletic show company, you might send promotions tied to large athletic events. If you're a toy store chain, you might ramp up your coupons during the holidays. Having a reason for sending the coupon makes it much more relevant to the consumer.

Enhance Messaging With Videos

Everyone likes viewing videos. You can use them to better explain products, services, almost anything. The key is to keep your videos concise and only send quality videos to your app users. In our age of YouTube and smartphones with built-in high-resolution cameras, app users expect and recognize quality.

> **"Today's Media-Oriented Consumers Are Accustomed To Having Instant Access To Rich Media"**

Mobile App Brand Guidelines

Branding. You know, that thing your business spent tons of money on so that everyone knows who you are - your name, your product, and your essence.

So if branding is so important, why are so many brands getting it wrong with their mobile apps? It can't be stressed enough: Mobile App Brand Guidelines must be established. Your guidelines should have the same clear creative rules as your brand's standard style guide including: color palette, logo usage, naming conventions and font. Above all, the guidelines should be platform-specific and always current in the rapidly evolving mobile platform landscape.

Providing guidance for mobile apps ensures they're not orphans in the plethora of advertising and marketing tools used to attract, engage and retain your customers.

Use High-End Graphics To Maximize Your Brand Image

Appropriate graphics are particularly adept at quickly and effectively communicating a brand's image. However, if you want your mobile apps to positively reflect upon your brand and/or match existing campaigns, quality graphics are critical. They need to match the sophistication consumers have come to expect from you and your branding.

Icons And Your Logo

Integrating your logo into your icon isn't a requirement for your app. But if you have an easily recognizable logo, it's a great way to gain immediate recognition from your customers. Google does an excellent job of designing an icon that fits within the construct of an app icon and conveys the meaning simultaneously (hello, Starbucks, Target, Redbox).

Useful Tips For Successful Mobile App Branding

It is understood and widely acknowledged by small business owners all over the world, that they need to market and hard sell their apps in order to succeed. But how does one get started with all this? How can you become successful in this mobile app branding venture?

One has to understand that rushing ahead and crafting a mobile application for a single or multiple platforms may not work out to be the best solution for your company, marketing-wise. It is also important to know that no single platform can be right for all mobile app brands.

3 Types Of Mobile App Brands.

1. Mobile Web apps exist to give the user a better browsing experience. Google Maps is a good example of a successful app brand.//
2. Apps such as Shazam, Foursquare and so on did very well in the market because they offered

something that users had never before experienced on their mobile devices.

3. Traditional app brands that have been around for a long time and keep delivering consistently good performance to users.

Any brand needs to focus on its customers, if it has to succeed in the market. In order to be able to capture maximum user attention, a mobile app has to be consistent with users' expectations of the claims made by the company and deliver a quality user experience as well.

Here is what you can do to achieve success with mobile app branding:

1. Remember, the consumer is King. It is of course important that your app is fun to use, but it should also be of utility value to the customer. Your customer is the key here and nothing else is more important than him/her.

2. You need to analyze the users' needs and motives for using the app and then make a marketing and branding plan accordingly.

3. Take into consideration the strengths and weaknesses of all the mobile platforms you are creating the app for. Each mobile platform behaves differently, so plan your app functionality accordingly.

4. Test your app thoroughly before submitting it to an app store. An app that crashes or freezes frequently can spell disaster for its own brand image.

5. Any mobile application can be effective in the market only and only if it offers something unique to the customer. In these days of competition, the customer can easily get what he/she is looking for online. In such a case scenario, your app brand can survive only if it can engage the user, while also being usable and consistent with the promises your company makes about it.

6. Once the previous step is done, you will have to set media and other marketing support plans in motion. Getting an app into the market without giving it enough marketing support is a sure-fire way to get it bombed, so marketing is an essential component of branding your mobile app.

7. Make your app easily referable to your users' friends. This way, your app stays in people's minds much longer than usual and also helps get your app higher ratings. The higher the positive rating, the more popularity and attention it will win in the market.

8. Providing frequent updates for your app goes a long way to help with mobile app branding, as keeps it fresh in the eyes of the consumer. Therefore, keep adding data and functionalities to it, as and when possible.

CHAPTER 5

INCREASING SALES WITH MOBILE APPS

This chapter illustrates some ways you might use mobile apps to increase sales. We've seen all these best practices successfully implemented by major brands. Essentially, they apply proven marketing and advertising principles to mobile apps, and help integrate all your marketing efforts.

> **"Imagine The Potential Customer... Interactively Selecting And Customizing Additional Products On His Or Her Smartphone"**

Showcasing Products And Services

Lure Consumers With A Mobile Product Showroom

Imagine a paper or online catalog. Now imagine the same catalog on your phone's screen with one critical difference: the ability to dynamically change products to your liking, save your preferences, and even return later to modify your selections.

For example, a furniture store might create a mobile app showing users photos of their product line. Consumers select furniture that interests them, say a chair, causing a new screen to open that displays a menu of the chairs available. The consumer then drills down further to examine detailed information about a particular chair.

As the engagement level rises, mobile users are able to add desired furniture to a favorites list or request directions to your nearest store to purchase items.

Better yet, imagine the potential customer in your retail store, interactively selecting and customizing additional products on his or her smartphone. With the help of your sales and customer service staff, customers can use the app at point of sale to finalize purchases.

And if you include the "Tell a Friend" feature mentioned earlier, this customer might refer another customer to your retail location.

Capture Leads While Increasing Engagement

For years, marketers have been developing sophisticated lead generation and database tools for capturing consumer and business leads. Yet, until now, other media channels have not been able to offer an integrated, highly engaging way to generate quality leads. Mobile has changed everything.

By using interactive elements rather than fill-in forms within the app, you encourage mobile users through widgets to provide lead capture information while increasing engagement. Although you can collect lead information with forms, widgets are more interactive and fun and generate higher compliance among mobile app users. Rich interactive widgets within apps are invaluable to marketers, advertisers, and brands.

> **"Users Have More Fun. And They Increasingly Become Engaged With Your Brand And App"**

In the furniture app we discussed earlier, an interactive "color consultant" encourages users to choose different room backgrounds, wall colors, pillows, sofas, and so forth. As the user makes changes, the app displays them in real time.

When finished, app users can save their designs, return to the app later, or even schedule an appointment with a color consultant at a local retail store to make a purchase. Meanwhile, you've captured the user's name, phone number, email address, preferences, and other information approved by the user when opting-in.

You've also captured their color preferences so you can offer them matching items and better choices when they visit your retail location.

Users have more fun. And they increasingly become engaged with your brand and app, which boosts sales. You've also captured valuable lead information for future contacts with your prospects and customers.

The Power Of Push Notifications

Mobile marketing is one of the fastest growing forms of marketing for small businesses, and the trend shows no signs of stopping due to powerful features such as push notifications.

So to start, what are push notifications?

If you download and use mobile apps, you've definitely seen these messages. Push notifications are instant alerts that show up in real time on a user's mobile device to communicate a small message. You know those pop-ups that show a red number next to your mobile apps? Yup, those are push notifications! These notifications are being used by a large variety of businesses to improve customer communication with great success.

When the alert displays on a mobile screen, users can see your new message or content with a single button press. This is a great way to drive people back into the app as well as test offers. If you provide good navigation and test offers, you'll engage consumers in your products or services. You'll find, that in many cases mobile app users appreciate notifications, especially if there's a special discount that ends soon.

According to global-marketing company Responsys, surveyed 1,200 adults and discovered that six out of 10 adults have downloaded apps from their preferred brands. Of those, seven in 10 have enabled push notifications for those apps. When a younger set of people were surveyed, those percentages grew.

According to the survey, users enabled push notifications for the following reasons:

- 50% for getting access to special or exclusive offers,
- 44% to keep track of orders
- 38% to review and manage accounts
- 36% to access brands on the go
- 34% to receive notifications in real time about sales and availability
- 31% to look up inventory
- 29% to stay up to date with products and services
- 28% to receive location based notifications
- 25% to better their website experience

In-app notifications are being used a great deal, with 68% having enabled notifications for their apps, and 76% of the younger age range (18-34) having done so. The survey showed that 70% of consumers surveyed said that in-app push notifications were valuable to them, 43% of consumers said they were more likely to use a mobile app when push notifications were available.

The statistics don't lie. Push notifications are a huge part of apps and mobile marketing now, and businesses should take note. This means huge return on investment for small businesses!

Collect Data For Profiling Further Marketing

Mobile apps offer an ideal environment for gathering information from the end user. Over time, you collect invaluable demographic and behavioral data about application users to help you plan new campaign strategies.

The more data you collect, the better you'll understand your app audience's preferences. To increase the demographic information you collect and drive respondents to your landing pages, you might offer discounts or awards for answering questions. A 15% off coupon for a limited time, for instance, will boost customer demographic statistics, providing you with a greater understanding of your customers.

Reviewing mobile analytics is the second step after collecting valuable data. According to Bango, a mobile analytics company, one study revealed that 83% of brands don't use mobile---specific analytic tools, which leads to inaccurate campaign performance data. 17% use some sort of measurement and 27%—around a third—don't measure at all.

Before launching and setting goals for your mobile app, make sure you have a way to measure user behavior.

> **"Mobile Apps Offer An Ideal Environment For Gathering Information From The End User"**

Boost Your App's Reach With Viral Marketing

For the purposes of this book, we'll define viral marketing as the sharing of content that is easily sent. That content might include a reposting of an offer, the spreading of your brand message, the forwarding of a discount, or the sharing of a customized brand experience.

The success of viral marketing in an app depends on both the content and how easily it can be shared. When creating an app for this purpose, you want to ensure that users can easily share it with all their contacts through a simple action. The great advantage of having users share your content is that you are essentially recruiting them to market your product or service. The branding potential here is limitless, and the return on your marketing dollars can be quite significant if you virally enable your app.

If you've targeted and reached your intended audience with mobile apps, it's quite likely that you'll attract additional consumers with profiles similar to your target audience when users send text messages or emails to their friends. This could potentially lower your marketing costs and boost ROI.

Using this best practice through a mobile app also means you're more likely to reach your targeted prospects and customers anytime and anywhere - a significant advantage over other media.

Befriend Social Networks To Reach More Consumers

Social networks, such as Twitter, Facebook, Instagram, and Snapchat are easily combined with mobile applications.

If your brand already has a strong social networking presence, your app can automatically use existing content you've previously created rather than authoring new content from scratch.

Through your app, you can also encourage users to upload and share content from your app to their social networks. Content that already resonates with your app's users will incite them to upload their ideas and respond in their social networks. This interactivity between your app and users' social networking sites increases the number of consumers your message can reach.

> **"Integrating Your Social Media Marketing With Mobile Applications Further Engages People Interested In Your Brand Or Company"**

As a brand, you'll want to share information and photos and encourage mobile users to share their opinions about your products with friends. Suggest they get feedback about potential purchases from their social network. App users will appreciate the interaction because they're clearly already engaged with your company.

Think back to the furniture brand example. Mobile app users could choose different furniture— chairs, tables, etc.—then drag and drop them around a photo of the room they want to furnish. This helps them see how selected furniture would look in their own homes.

Once they're done, they can save it or upload it to a social network, ask their friends' opinions about the furniture, and get feedback. You might even suggest in your text messages that app users post their selections on your Facebook brand page to share their choices with more people. Comments made by Facebook members who are members of your group increase the viral effect and may create new friends.

As you can see, integrating your social media marketing with mobile applications further engages people interested in your brand or company.

"Bridge The Gap Between Physical And Digital"

Mobile Apps Are The New Loyalty Cards

"Loyalty" has always been something marketers – and businesses – care about. Why else do we tell each other (truthfully) that "it costs 10 times as much to acquire one new customer as it does to keep an existing one"? Because we understand, at least when we stop to think about it, that it's just as important to hold on to our existing users or customers as it is to acquire new ones.

And why else do so many businesses spend so much money on loyalty schemes of one description or another? From the nakedly commercial (supermarket loyalty schemes) to more 'soft' loyalty programs (the local coffee shop remembering your name, or a bar offering you a free beer), in one way or another well run businesses have ways to keep you coming back. And if they don't, they won't be in business for long.

Enter The Mobile App

Of course in the digital landscape, we've become accustomed to seeing our competition as 'one click away' – and that has colored our whole approach to loyalty online. That's why most digital businesses have a variety of more-or-less sophisticated techniques designed to keep customers engaged and bring them back if they have left (or appear to have left).

But the mobile app changes that. Let's make it clear:

The mobile app is the single greatest loyalty factor in digital business today

A bold claim for sure. But there's absolutely no doubt it is true. Consider the reality of the consumer's digital landscape today. To all intents and purposes, they have a small computer they carry with them all day, look at or use at least 100 times a day, and use to access almost every service they need at any moment in time.

They also display a marked preference for mobile apps, with app traffic now dominating mobile Internet use to the tune of 5:1 or so.

All that creates a situation whereby if the provider of a particular service has their app on my home screen, **it is almost inevitable that I will use that provider when I require the service.** Whether that's booking a table in a restaurant or a flight, ordering a taxi, or shopping for groceries – that should be obvious.

That in turn means the following:

Getting on, and staying on, the smartphone screen is the single most important thing your business can do to improve customer loyalty today.

Making It Happen

That's the 'good' news. The bad news, of course, is that staying on that screen is hard. Of course it is, in a world populated by millions of apps, and where something like 20% of all app installs are used once, and it is not unusual to lose over 50% of all app users within a week of install. So although the huge amounts of acquisition spend we see in the market are justified in one sense (we understand how important the mobile app is to the business), in other ways much of it is wasted. We are spending money on new users who never convert into valuable customers.

By making your mobile loyalty programs an extension of your physical one, you ensure customers always have their loyalty cards with them because they're on their phones.

You'll benefit from less lost sales and more frequent use of your app. A current trend is integrating loyalty programs with location sharing. This has been adopted by brands using the check-in model.

Making the program fun, utilizing game mechanics and altering the rules will also keep your app lively and interesting to users.

These types of mobile programs recognize the nature of the mobile channel. It's the most personalized medium yet invented and continues to grow at an extraordinary rate.

Businesses that understand this highly personalized communication tool are likely to benefit the most from their loyalty programs.

Sticky Apps Ensure Long Term Success

Designing and building an app is the easy part. Creating an app that highly engages users so they constantly think about your brand and use the app is the greater challenge. If you can accomplish this, you've got a "sticky app." Like a blog or website, fresh, exciting, and useful content brings readers back to your site and convinces them to subscribe to your RSS feed.

However, the importance of strategic planning, when it comes to apps is often overlooked by marketers, advertisers and brand managers. Like a newsletter, you wouldn't haphazardly write one without a strategy. You plan the layout, content and release dates to integrate the newsletter into your overall marketing strategies and goals. This increases the open rate and encourages content sharing, which in turn exposes more people to your brand.

> **"Typical Mobile Users Remove An App From Their Phones Within 24 Hours If They're Not Immediately Turned On By Its Usefulness"**

Mobile apps aren't any different. Mobile users, in many cases, have dozens of apps on their smartphones and will remove those with the least appeal very quickly. In fact, typical mobile users remove an app from their phones within 24 hours if they're not immediately turned on by its usefulness. To make your app stick and encourage repeated use, you need to convince users of its usefulness.

This takes much prior planning, and should involve consultations with expert mobile app designers who understand how to maximize an app's marketing potential for your benefit.

The success of your push notifications is also dependent on your app's stickiness. Push notifications are the purest form of direct marketing. The moment you present your offer, consumers can take advantage of it with one button press.

Ensure App Stickiness And Success With These Strategies

In this book, we've presented several best practices that will help you avoid losing your app devotees. While designing your app, determine how often content will be updated and pushed out to your users. Incorporate push notifications that pop up on mobile screens and show users the title of the app so they can choose to view the message or dismiss it. These features will enhance your app's attractiveness.

Further ensure your app sticks by keeping your content fresh, interesting, and engaging. Like a newsletter or series of emails, you're addressing different audiences and need to segment your lists so that messages are sent to the right target audience at the right time. Metrics from your results will help you design successful push campaigns and increase the percentage of users who read your new content.

As you become more familiar with your mobile audience through feedback, keeping your app "sticky" will become easier.

Additionally, don't rely on your mobile app alone. Integrate your app strategy with online, email, print, broadcast, and other media. Email and print are great places to tell people about your fantastic new mobile application. Describe how the app will benefit users. Encourage them to download your app to get a discount coupon or useful information.

Mention how newsletter subscribers will benefit through continuously updated product and service information. You can't engage app users if they're not using your app. So the first step is promoting your app in other media.

> **"Don't Rely On Your Mobile App Alone. Integrate Your App Strategy With Online, Email, Print, Broadcast, And Other Media"**

CHAPTER 6

CONCLUSION

Choosing A Mobile App Solution Provider

Finally, you'll want to work with an experienced mobile application development company. Consulting with professionals who have extensive experience designing mobile applications for many industries will save you time and eliminate wasted efforts.

The importance of consulting mobile app professionals cannot be stressed. These solution providers have the expertise to effectively strategize and design a mobile app that successfully represents your brand and delivers relevant content. They know how to create mobile user interfaces that quickly procure app store approval and don't upset customers.

Their creativity will take advantage of smartphone features to develop an optimal marketing experience that's fun and engaging for the end user. Mobile app solution providers understand this unique media.

When choosing a provider, you'll want to consider a few things. In addition to the company's track record and portfolio, you'll want a provider that speaks your language and understands your business goals. The provider should be asking you questions. Moreover, they should not push their sole solution, but instead offer various ways to integrate your mobile app with other marketing programs you may have in place. Most of all, you want to be comfortable with your mobile app provider. Good communication between client and provider always leads to more effective results.

Conclusion

Most of us do not remember the times when we had to make do without our trustworthy mobile apps. These are the times to pick up your smartphone to look up the next best eatery, from helping you travel easily, to waking you up in the morning, from sending your photos to someone on the other side of the world in a matter of minutes, to helping you perfect your lasagna, we all turn to our trusted mobile applications to help us out. Mobile applications have brought to us a new and exciting social and cultural experience that continues to fascinate us.

A number of small businesses are reaching out to making their own apps since apps have proven to be very effective in providing the ability to reach customers 24 X 7. They help stay on-par and ahead, at times, of the competition as they help you tap into new sales channels very easily.

Mobile apps also provide a wealth of opportunities. To ensure your mobile app is a success and your campaign creates a viral effect, follow the pointers discussed in this book. Use strong messaging and content relevant to your brand; ensure you maximize mobile device capabilities through excellent technical development; understand mobile user interfaces to expedite app store approval and maintain good relationships with your customers; ensure optimal marketing results through excellent mobile creative elements; and keep focusing on fun and engaging experiences for your end users.

The app economy has started to boom and everyone from small scale to multination businesses have started understanding and accepting the need to have their name pinned on an app. From companies that are inching upwards to meet the demands of technology driven market to the sheer number of opportunities unleashed by the mobile industry – mobile business apps are able to improve productivity, improve customer service, support sales and marketing, bring in newer and more reliable leads, and give access to a wide range of target audiences. Mobile apps seem to be poised to become the next growth engine that us ready to turn the world of business economy into something more vibrant, innovative and full of interesting opportunities.

As more people turn to their phones for information, companies need to be mobile ready. Success will hinge on understanding this nuanced technology and developing an overall mobile strategy to guide mobile campaigns. Smart mobile apps can solve many issues for brands, enhance the buying experience and provide great return on marketing dollars. For optimum success, consult mobile app experts.

If you have any mobile app development related questions or wish to set up a free no obligation consultation I am available! Please do no hesitate to contact me.

To Your Success!

Kyle D. Amaker
CEO at MobileFusionSoft.com, Inc

CHAPTER 7

ABOUT MOBILEFUSIONSOFT.COM, INC

What We Do

We are an in-house mobile app development and design studio specializing in small businesses. Our apps are designed and developed to help you increase sales, grow your business, attract new customer, and retain exiting customers.

Bottom line we love mobile. We live mobile. We understand mobile. We've been working in mobile for over 5 years. We're passionate about creating engaging interactive solutions and delivering great user experiences.

Specifically, we harness our mobile savvy to design and develop strategically integrated mobile experiences; direct product creation, innovation, and ideation; and help companies maximize mobile opportunities.

When it comes to creating rich mobile marketing, we insist on clean design, effective user interfaces, and great experiences. MobileFusionSoft.com, Inc specialties include:

- **iPhone, iPad & Android apps** – effectively engage consumers and build your brand
- **Mobile Sites & Landing Pages** – drive business and elicit immediate action
- **Mobile Rich Media Ads** – promote your messaging and products 24/7
- **SMS Text Messaging** – communicate with your clients via text messaging

We've been creating rich mobile experiences since 2011 and believe your projects deserve outstanding results. We also know it's our job to make your life easier, make you successful, and increase your profits. For help on a mobile project or to learn more about our services, please visit **www.MobileFusionSoft.com** You may also contact us at **(800) 951-5632** or email us at **Info@MobileFusionSoft.com**.

Our Services

Our services are delivered by our team with years of experience. We are passionate about providing mobile solutions for small businesses.

Mobile Advertising

It is extremely critical for business owners to have more direct access to their customers and to be able to drum-up more business when needed. Pay-Per-Click advertising has the potential to generate sales and revenues for your business if properly utilized.

Small Business Apps

Do you have an iPhone or Android phone, or have you spent any time around someone who does? Then you've undoubtedly got a feel for how addictive apps can be. Now, creating your own app can be a great way for your small business to attract customers.

SMS Text Messaging

The huge volume of text messages already surpass that of mobile voice calls. And, getting just a small portion of that volume by using targeted text message advertising is something your business must consider if you are to compete in today's market.

INDUSTRIES WE SERVICE

WE CREATE CUSTOM MOBILE APPS FOR BUSINESSES ACROSS A WIDE VARIETY OF INDUSTRIES!

CAR DEALERSHIPS

More and more customers are choosing to start their shopping process at the dealership through the smartphone. Smartphone shoppers can interact with your individual inventory through their smartphone, receive information, offers, or specials, tied specifically to the vehicle they are in front of.

- Lock mobile customers into your dealership early in the sales process
- Generate additional traffic & leads from mobile shoppers
- Schedule more service appointments from customers on the go

Why Your Car Dealership Needs A Mobile App

- 59% of shoppers used their smartphone to research prior to visiting a dealership

- 25% of people used only their smartphone to conduct research prior to visiting a dealership

- 62% of shoppers will visit an additional dealership within the next 24 hours.

"If You're Not On Mobile You're Not Competing"

CHURCHES

Considering the fact that 66% of Americans own smartphones, allowing your congregation to access your church information via a mobile app is a huge benefit.

- Add your sermons existing RSS feed and have your church app updated automatically
- Keep your congregation up to date! Post church wide events.
- Integrate the churches Facebook and Twitter post directly within the app
- Prayer Wall allows your congregation to stay connected in prayer
- Add your existing online giving platform
- Take your print materials digital

Why Your Church Needs A Mobile App

A church app offers unlimited benefits and is the most effective communication tool in staying engaged with your congregation.

Mobile apps account for 91% of all mobile internet traffic with two thirds of the average congregation owning smart phones. Apps are not a fad but an integral part of any progressive church.

FITNESS CLUBS

Need to hassle your students about showing up to that 7am boot camp? No better way than through a push notification. Post class schedules, send out last-minutes updates and generate feedback all in one place.

- Integrate your online class schedule
- Offer mobile discounts and app-only coupons
- Post workout videos and playlists
- Share exercise tips in a variety of formats
- Sell gear and company merchandise in-app
- Generate client feedback
- Promote your business with sharing features

Why Your Fitness Club Needs A Mobile App

Resolution-chasers and gym rats alike need a way to plug in. Signing someone up for a monthly membership doesn't seal the deal, especially in a highly competitive industry like fitness.

It's critical that your club stick out in the crowd, and offering mobile promotions, progress-tracking and nutrition & workout info helps you stay ahead of the game.

HAIR SALONS BARBER SHOPS

Let's cut right to the chase: having a mobile app can help you get more customers, book more appointments and increase revenue. For many small businesses, a mobile app is a great new way to connect with customers and open new marketing channels. But for hair salons and barbershops in particular, mobile apps offer a bunch of great features to boost business cost-effectively.

- Mobile Reservations
- Appointment Reminders
- Style Libraries
- Special Offers
- Loyalty Programs
- Customer Photos

Why Your Hair Salon Needs A Mobile App

With a mobile app dedicated to your business, you will unlock the power of customer retention and repeat business.

The probability of selling to an existing customer is 60-70%. The probability of selling to a new prospect is 5-20%.

REALTORS

Place your listings in the palm of buyers' hands. With in-depth property info and on-the-go contact capabilities, you'll be selling houses up from under people's feet. Add photos and listing details so users are ready to buy before they reach the front door.

- Add need property listings daily
- Broadcast open house dates
- Customize click-to-call and email features
- Give one-touch directions
- Sync up YouTube channels for virtual tours
- Calculate mortgage rates right through the app
- Showcase the neighborhood hotspots

Why Realtors Need A Mobile App

Listings are the main reason that real estate companies develop apps, but that isn't all. You can use them for marketing and promotions too.

Using geofencing and push notifications, you'll recruit new clients right from the app, based on their own needs, interest and location.

"If You're Not On Mobile You're Not Competing"

RESTAURANTS

It's easy to draw the Monday night crowd when you have an app working for you. Check-in specials, loyalty rewards, and real-time menu updates grow your customer base and keep them coming back for seconds. Dessert menu, please.

- Accept orders and payment in-app
- Highlight weekly specials
- Reward your regulars with check-in discounts
- Send targeted push notifications to nearby users
- Post about your favorite dish on the fan wall
- Give directions & quick contact for users on the go
- Enable in-app reservations-booking

Why Your Restaurant Needs A Mobile App

Mobile apps are empowering the food service industry to create dining experiences that are simple and convenient.

These dining experiences include:

1. Customers can set up reservations on their mobile device.
2. Ordering online is simple with mobile apps.
3. Billing is more convenient than ever before.

RETAIL

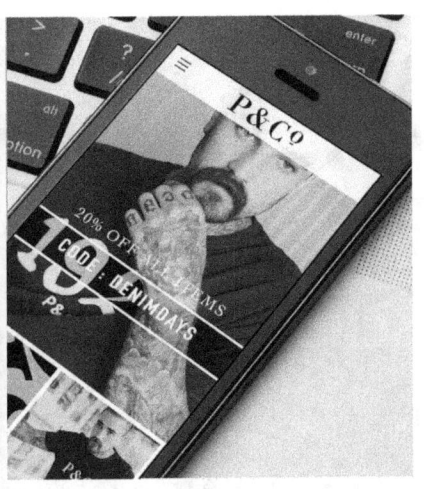

From store locator, products, offers and loyalty information to quick check out process, a consumer facing branded mobile app for your retail chain can help you completely transform the in-store experiences and increase sales.

- Allow users to shop within your app
- Stay in contact with your customers by gathering their names & emails directly inside the app.
- Loyalty program
- List your weekly specials or upcoming events with the Event feature
- Display pictures of your business, menu items, or photos from past events with the Gallery feature

Why Your Retail Business Needs A Mobile App

- 47% of shoppers want real-time promotions

- Only 16% of retailers can automatically credit coupons and discounts.

- 57% of users are willing to share data to get access to promotions and coupons.

SCHOOLS

The clear and timely sharing of information between schools and their families is vital for efficient and cohesive education. By improving school parent communication, a mobile app has a host of benefits for both parties.

- Parent involvement, engaging parents with the school, keeping parents connected.
- Going green (less paper, less repetitive notices)
- Provides at your fingertips communication and engagement for all parents 24/7
- Time sensitive updates and emergency broadcast via instant messages (push notifications)

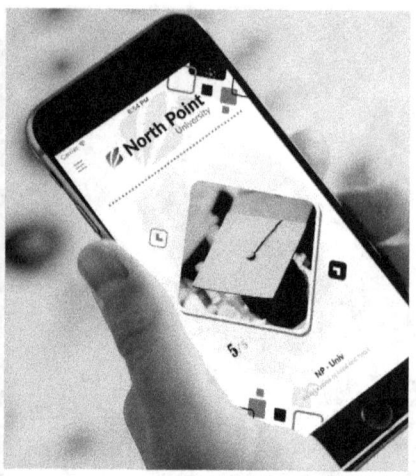

Why Your School Needs A Mobile App

As more and more schools now have blogs and websites, it gives both parents and students the ability to stay up to date with events and information that the school puts out.

The availability of a school app lets the school increase its availability and accessibility to parents, which is very important.

APP FUNCTIONALITY

POWERFUL MOBILE APP FEATURES FOR YOUR BUSINESS

Around Us

The Around Us feature is a great way to display relevant points of interest within your app, drawing attention to hotspots in the area.

Contact

Give customers multiple ways to contact your business. Phone, website, email, and directions to your business..

Push Notifications

Send messages to your customers whenever you'd like using our easy to use content management system.

Email Form

The email form feature allows you to create a custom form for soliciting customer feedback, taking appointments requests, and gathering info from users.

Email Photo

Allow customers to take a photo or send an existing photo and email it directly to your business.

Events

Let users notify others they are attending any event inside of your mobile app.

Events v2

Include all of your business events inside of your application. Keep customers informed on the go.

Fan Wall

Set up a fan wall for your customers to leave feedback on your business. Manage the comments online.

Food Ordering

Allow restaurant customers to place food orders directly inside the mobile app or mobile website.

"If You're Not On Mobile You're Not Competing"

Golf Courses

With the golf course feature, you can build out a golf course range and allow users to score their games right in the app.

GPS Coupon

Create mobile coupons for your customers to unlock by "checking in" at your business.

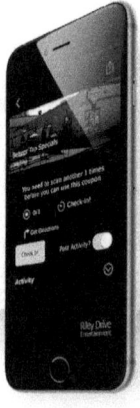

Image Gallery

Display images of your business in a beautiful image gallery specifically optimized for the iPhone and Android.

Info-1-Tier

The Info-1-Tier feature is a single static HTML page where you can insert just about anything that you can insert on a regular web page.

Info-2-Tier

The Info-1-Tier feature is multiple static HTML pages defined by category where you can insert just about anything as if it were a regular web page.

Info-3-Tier

The Info-1-Tier feature is multiple static HTML pages defined by category and subcategory where you can insert just about anything as if it were a regular web page.

Loyalty

Reward loyal customers for making frequent visits or purchases at your small business.

Mailing List

Stay in contact with your customers by gathering names and email addresses directly inside your application.

Membership

This feature can be a great way for exclusive groups to create mobile apps for their audience.

Menu

Upload photos and descriptions of food or services found on the menu for your business.

Merchandise

Start making sales through your app by creating your own marketplace or opt to integrate a service such as Magento or Shopify.

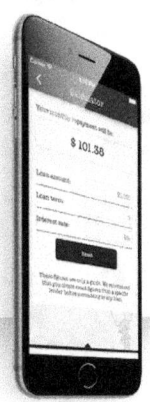

Mortgage Calculator

Include a mortgage calculator feature where you can preset the interest rate. Perfect for real estate agents.

Music

Give your fans and customer the ability to listen to & purchase music inside your app.

News

Easily gather content instantly from Twitter, Google News, and Facebook in seconds with our powerful News Feature.

Notepad

The notepad feature allows users to record text notes and email them to anyone at any time.

PDF

The PDF feature allows you to display PDFs through your app. This is commonly used to showcase flyers, menus, and even reports.

Podcast

Engage users with your podcasts. Stream podcasts inside of your mobile app for your users to listen at their leisure.

QR Coupon

Create QR enabled coupons for your customers to redeem at your business by scanning a specified QR code.

QR Scanner

The QR Scanner allows your users to scan any QR code they happen to come across.

Real Estate

Engage users with your podcasts. Stream podcasts inside of your mobile app for your users to listen at their leisure.

Reservation

Use our custom booking system or integrate with a 3rd party like MindBody to allow users to reserve time slots for various services.

RSS Feed

RSS feeds are a popular form of displaying news and information. RSS feeds load a web page that constantly updates with new content.

Sports Stats

The Sports Stats feature allows you to include a flexible counter inside your app.

Tell Friend

Let your customers take your business viral with built in sharing capabilities over email, Facebook, SMS, and Twitter.

Tip Calc

Include a tip calculator inside your app to help customers quickly calculate a tip amount for a dinner party.

Voice Recording

The voice recorder feature allows users to record voice notes and email them to anyone at any time.

Web Site

The Web Site feature allows you to easily integrate any mobile friendly web page into your app allowing users a great deal of flexibility and customization.

WuFoo Form

Easily create an appointment, order, feedback or contact form using WuFoo and much much more.

YouTube Channel

Easily display hundreds of videos from your YouTube channel beautifully inside of your mobile apps.

One Touch Calling

Give your customers one touch calling from inside your app. No numbers to save or remember.

Video Integration

Integrate your YouTube channel in a beautifully displayed format for your customers.

Direction View

The Direction View feature offers one-touch directions to multiple locations.

3rd Party Integrations

Easily Incorporate Best In Class 3rd Party Tools And Services

Food Ordering
- MyCheckApp.com
- OnlineOrdering.com
- OlO.com
- Eat24.com
- GrubHub.com
- Seamless.com
- Onosys.com

Email
- MyEmma.com
- CampaignMonitor.com
- ConstantContact.com
- GetResponse.com
- iContact.com
- MailChimp.com
- Wufoo.com

Multimedia
- SoundCloud.com
- Instagram.com
- Picasa.Google.com
- YouTube.com
- Flickr.com

Reservations
- OpenTable.com
- MindBodyOnline.com
- FrontDeskHQ.com

- BookSteam.com
- Groupon.com

E-Commerce
- Shopify.com
- Magento.com
- Volusion.com

Request A Free Custom Mobile App Demo

As a business owner, it's important to recognize that your customers have already gone mobile...meaning they're using their mobile devices to browse websites for information.

Now, more than ever, it's essential that you show customers that marketing your business and services to them creates a true mobile-friendly experience when viewing your business on a smart phone...

Our FREE custom mobile app demo will highlight the benefits of a mobile app, providing the total solution to easily view your business on the mobile devices of your customers...

Big Businesses are paying roughly **$4K** just to see what an App can look like for their business. Add to that another **$50K+** to develop a Mobile App for iPhone and Android.

But you don't have to! We will make your company a **FREE Custom Mobile App Demo** complete with interactive features and a custom design. There is no cost for this service.

To Take Advantage Of This Limited Time Offer!

Go To: MobileFusionSoft.com
Or Give Us A Call At (800) 951-5632

FAQ

THE MOST ASKED QUESTIONS FROM OUR CUSTOMERS

"If You're Not On Mobile You're Not Competing"

Frequently Asked Questions

The Most Asked Questions. Here Are Some Of The Most Frequent Questions That Our Experts Answered For Our Customers.

Q. How long does it take from design to build and approve a mobile app in the app stores?

A. Around 3-4 weeks from start to finish after we have agreed on your mobile app design including approval from Apple and the Google play store.

Q. How will my customers get to know about my mobile app once it has gone live in the app stores?

A. We can help you with offline and online marketing strategies that will help your branded mobile app to be visible in your business category as well as in the pockets of your customers.

Q. Don't people spend more of their time on a mobilized website or desktop computer than on a mobile app?

A. Mobile app users are more engaged as on average they have 2.4 times more impressions than mobile web users. Mobile app users spend 94 minutes per day when mobile website users spend only 72 minutes per day.

Q. **Can I advertise Apple and Google Play app logos in my shop front and on hard copy marketing like flyers?**

A. Credibility of your business with Apple and Google puts your brand up there with the best. Yes we can help you include these on all electronic and printed communications, such as TV commercials, print ads, video trailers, email, newsletters, and websites.

Q. **I have more than one location for my business. Is it possible to have multiple locations built into the app?**

A. We can integrate all locations into your app as it's designed. Even if you decided at a later stage that you needed another shop or business location, we can do this for you at an agreed cost that wouldn't require a full design and build.

Q. **Is my mobile app free to download from the Apple and Google Play app stores for all my customers?**

A. Yes your mobile app is completely free for your customers to download from the Apple and Google Play app stores.

Q. **After my one-time app design and development fee, are there any other charges that I have to pay for?**

A. If you like the free custom mobile app that we developed for you and you would like to move forward with our services. There will be a one-time app design and development fee.

Also just like any other professional business website there are monthly costs. Its the same with your mobile app. Monthly hosting and updates will be required to keep your mobile app safely hosted in the cloud using the safest technology with 99.9% premium uptime.

Q. **Are your app design and development fees competitive?**

A. Mobile app development is not cheap. Our mobile app service is but a mere fraction of the price of a custom developed mobile app. On average, for example, a restaurant can spend upwards of $20,000 spending many months on development for a fairly basic app with other app developers. We can develop a professional mobile app in weeks using our service.

Q. **What if I decide that I don't need my mobile app for my business any more after my app has gone live in the app stores?**

A. There are no contracts after your first month of your completed mobile app. If you decide to stop your monthly hosting and updates, we would cancel your subscription and remove your app from our cloud hosting and your app will no longer show in the app stores.

www.ingramcontent.com/pod-product-compliance
Lightning Source LLC
Chambersburg PA
CBHW070258190526
45169CB00001B/464